SAY IT, SOW IT, GROW IT, SUSTAIN IT

SAY IT, SOW IT, GROW IT, SUSTAIN IT

Regina Reed

xulon press

Xulon Press
2301 Lucien Way #415
Maitland, FL 32751
407.339.4217
www.xulonpress.com

Due to the changing nature of the Internet, if there are any web addresses, links, or URLs included in this manuscript, these may have been altered and may no longer be accessible. The views and opinions shared in this book belong solely to the author and do not necessarily reflect those of the publisher. The publisher therefore disclaims responsibility for the views or opinions expressed within the work.

Unless otherwise indicated, Scripture quotations taken from the Holy Bible, New International Version (NIV). Copyright © 1973, 1978, 1984, 2011 by Biblica, Inc.™. Used by permission. All rights reserved.

Paperback ISBN-13: 978-1-66284-796-7
Ebook ISBN-13: 978-1-66284-797-4

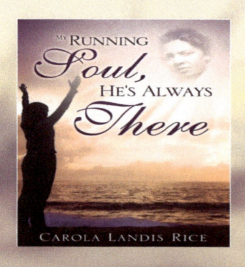

My RUNNING *Soul,* HE'S ALWAYS *There*

CAROLA LANDIS RICE

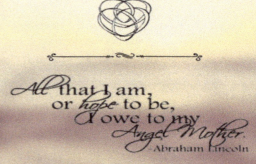

*All that I am,
or hope to be,
I owe to my
Angel Mother.*
-Abraham Lincoln

A SPECIAL THANK YOU

I would like to acknowledge my beautiful and extraordinary mother, author Carola Rice, for her unwavering advice, guidance, love, prayers, sacrifice, and invaluable support throughout my life. She is the sole reason why I am the woman I am today. Mommy, it's your prayers that have kept me from falling over that slippery slope – "thank you" is not enough. *BLESS YOU*!

I remember when you started writing your masterpiece (in May 2009). Right in the middle of you writing your beautiful story, you were admitted into the hospital. The devil thought he defeated you, but you flipped the script by tossing him back to his lil' home in the pit of hell. To God be the glory!

After sixteen days of being on life support, three whole months in the hospital, and a series of outside and in-home rehabilitation, you made it! So, I salute and dedicate this book to you for overcoming so many hard blows, twists, and turns throughout your life. To my readers, I encourage you to grab a copy of my mother's book 'My Running Soul, He's Always There'; it will move your soul!

"YOU CAN'T STOP ME FROM DREAMING, NO MATTER HOW HARD YOU TRY."

Regina Reed

Wife | Mother | Mentor | Servant | Wealth Coach

"The tongue has the power of life and death. The stakes are high. Your words can either speak life, or your words can speak death." – Proverbs 18:20-21

Table of Contents

Help me to always be mindful that You hear every word that comes out of my mouth. Make me quick to listen, slow to speak, and slow to anger – James 1:19

CHAPTER 1

What Did You Say?

Despite the forecast, live like it's Spring!

"Ma, there's something I need to tell you."

LET ME TELL you, when a mother is approached by her oldest son that he has some important news, it will leave you on edge. All I could do was lock eyes on him, as I held my breath in anticipation of the disclosure he was about to reveal. Time stood still as the afternoon unfurled its shadows across the shoulders of the Georgia sky. I knew my son was about to reveal something of enormous magnitude.

"I'm getting married!"

My entire body froze, and tears flowed down my face in excitement as my child leaned in to wrap his arms around me. As my sobs subsided, he proceeded to share with us the events leading up to his engagement. As he cried in my arms, my heart began to flutter in amazement. I verbally shouted, "It's time to plan a wedding!"

You might be asking, what does this announcement that her oldest son is getting married have to do with praying before you say it?

I'm glad you asked.

It is a simple formula, with powerful results:

Pause - > Pray - > Speak

The words you speak are calculated, and there is no better way to calculate our words than through prayer.

My prayer to God was to order my son's steps and position them to not only be successful in life, but to kneel before Him in prayer, and ask whatever was his heart's desire. Notably, following my prayer declaration, I seal it with faith. Faith isn't just a notion that some people hold onto in tough times; faith is an important element to all human life on earth. Faith is what helps you get through this journey called life, illuminating the pathway in times of darkness, and giving us strength in times of weakness. You see, faith is one of the cornerstones of your personal relationship with your spirituality. Without faith, we are lost.

> *"Having faith doesn't mean God will always change*
> *your situation. Sometimes, He changes you."*
> — *Steven Furtick*

CHAPTER 2

You Need to Pray Before You Speak

WHEN I STEPPED into the management role within my company in 1996, I was asked to tour a couple of pharmacies throughout our call center. My approach was all wrong. I was under the mistaken impression that in my new role, I needed to be seriously lacking in my flavor of authenticity and flamboyance. What I ended up doing was communicating our day-to-day operations in the most dull, stiff, and lifeless way possible. Based on the body language of some individuals, it must have felt like they were at a lecture. Looking back, I wish I had allowed myself to be me, and if I could replay that day again, I would have showed my unique personality. So, I vowed to make it my goal to fulfil God's mission through me, organically, with authenticity and humility.

Do you have anyone in your circle who always wants to be the center of attention, always making it about them? I ask that question somewhat jokingly because most people who continually embrace that posture don't tend to have very many close friends. They may have a few people here and there who graciously put up with them, but bragging is an effective way to repel people.

Sometimes, when the Lord does something good in our lives, we share that information. Other times, we choose not to because we're fearful of it coming across like we're bragging, but as one of the most notable apostles in the Bible demonstrates in this passage, there's nothing wrong with humbly letting others know about the ways in which the Lord is accomplishing His mission through you.

There were so many times throughout the course of my life when I became convinced that the Lord had caused something to work out well as a way of lending me His credibility. On many occasions, I have whispered this praise to the Lord: "Lord, thank you for having my back. I see what You're doing, and I appreciate it."

While I have breath in my body, I will make it my number one goal to preach the gospel where it needs to be heard. You see, everyone needs a Word and a touch from God during these challenging times. It's like how you eat an apple, one bite at a time. God requires us to take one step at a time.

If you fall seven times, get up on eight.

What are you going to do with what God has given you?

What are you going to do with your testimony?

Here's a fun fact: if you don't use what God has given you, you will lose it.

"Go to God in prayer before you open your mouth"

CHAPTER 3

Remain Vertical and in Position to Stay Blessed

QUITE OFTEN, I'VE been in the midst of situations where I found myself struggling to be 100% open and candid, in fear of hurting one's feelings. What I know to be true is that life is short. There is no time to leave important words unsaid. Words are powerful. A teenage girl in the Bible became pregnant, not by a man, but by a Word from God. The angel appeared to her and said, "You are highly favored! You will conceive and have a baby, without physically being with a man. He will be the Messiah, the Son of God." – Isaiah 7:14. When God wants to create, He doesn't use material things; He uses His Word.

Mary could have said to the angel, "That's impossible; it's never happened before." Instead, she said, "Be it unto me, even as you have said." – Luke 1:38 She got into agreement with God. She used her words to confirm, not debate what she had heard.

When the world tells us to stop serving and praising God, we need to pray even louder, because godly counsel and wisdom is paramount. It's a beautiful thing when you're in the right place at the right time. There are a lot of people that give credit to that word "luck," but it's nothing other than a divine appointment when, at the right season, God places His hand on you.

Here's a fun fact: when God's touch comes down on you, everybody around you will know it. When God blesses you, will see the anointing and favor all over you. Some of you may be asking why? Because God wants all the glory, and to those of you who yield yourself to Him, and embrace humbleness, God will position you to be used for His glory. Now, enemies are a part of your destiny. God will use your enemies to get you to your destiny. In this day and time, you must maintain unrestrained boldness. God wants to fill us so that He can use us!

When God puts a promise in your heart, my commission to you is get into agreement with Him. Speak your healing. Don't debate it. "I don't feel healed. My back is still sore," you might say. Get in a vertical position and begin speaking boldly. "Lord, thank You that I am healed. Be it unto me, even as You have said."

Sickness and disease cannot dwell in the same place where God dwells. Get your eyes off man and his limitations and keep your eyes on Jesus. Show the world evidence of the miracles, signs, and wonders from your prayer declaration right now. Get your heart and mind in alignment, and watch God change the situation around in your favor. Whenever there's opposition, pressure, and depression, get ready, you're about to witness the best season of your life!

> *"God continues to step up, when people who you thought were your friends stepped out!"*

CHAPTER 4

You've Got the Courage to Speak It into Existence

IN JULY OF 2021, Covid found its way into my home. Yes, something I couldn't see, feel, or touch had the audacity to take control of my entire body! During that period, tears flowed down my face, and not even to mention the agony I was in. I began to cancel out that spirit of helplessness and defeat and flip the script by calling on the name of Jesus!

Remember, you always have to look at what Scripture says about you. You've been designed for the journey. When you start seeing yourself as strong, empowered, able to do all things, then you won't be overwhelmed and out of sync, mentally and physically. You'll discover a strength that you didn't know you had.

It takes courage and spiritually connected divine power to walk into an atmosphere that is set against you. However, if you're going to get what you want out of life, out of God, in any adverse situation, you've got to be anointed, prepared, and stay in your Word while getting ready. People may be murmuring in corners, but you have to know that the mission you are on is so important that you cannot afford to worry about what people think, let alone what they say about you. It's time to stop hanging with negativity and worry and get into alignment with grace and mercy. You must block out that negativity, take up your cross, and go anyway.

It has been both a conviction and a thought of mine lately as to what it would look like to truly, relentlessly, and wholly live out what I say I believe. It's plainly obvious that I must make it a goal to dive deeper and deeper into the Bible, develop a more intimate relationship with Jesus, get to know Him more, and improve my literacy and understanding of His Word. But it always seems that whenever I come to a fork in the road in my walk with God, for some reason, I always choose the path of least resistance, which in turn, is mostly always the wrong path.

Maybe you can relate with me? Maybe your sticking point isn't insecurity, self-doubt, or the fact that you can't seem to let go of negative energy. Or maybe it's because you're complacent (with where you're at in your walk), or maybe it's selfishness. What if selfishness is manifesting itself in your life to the point where you feel like it's not your responsibility to speak out and share the Word with everyone you come into contact with? Here's a fun fact: it is our responsibility to share the Word! Are you courageous enough to walk into the unknown, and not make it about you?

All of us have a commission to do God's work in the earth. It's your turn; it's your time!

> *"Without commitment, you'll never start. Without consistency, you'll never finish." — Denzel Washington*

CHAPTER 5

Impact Over Income

EVERY MONDAY EVENING at 7:00 p.m., my oldest son hosts a Millionaire Mindset training with his team. During this one-hour training, he emphasizes the importance of preserving your mind, while knowing and understanding your primary role in your business. During one of our training sessions, he shared a powerful and compelling testimony where at the beginning stages of his business, his number one goal was to enroll a lot of clients and agents, so that he could reach his financial and title goals every month.

The competitive mindset that he embraced became short-lived when he realized that his number one desire to make a massive income ended up becoming a huge issue. He discovered that he never listened to the needs of his prospects during the initial consultation, which was a huge mistake. When he started his business in October of 2019, it was out of necessity because he was trading time for money, and he couldn't stand his job.

Why would anyone walk out of a job making a nice income, and start their own business where the income at the beginning was nowhere near what he was making in Corporate America?

He named a few reasons:

- Chasing income, not impacting people

- Scarcity mindset
- Building someone else's legacy, and not his own

Are you vicariously competing with your neighbor?

Do you have the capacity to help and serve someone in need?

Are you a three-dimensional thinker?

Are you empathetic?

Are you exchanging money for time and freedom, while creating a balance between your family and your clients?

Is your "Why?" compelling and strong enough?

In order to be a success story, passion needs to be your drive, ambition, and the love of what you do and who you serve. Having that passion provides you with a very special view of the world that others often don't see. Embrace and relish the business that God has blessed you with and replace your excuses with adjustments along the way. Now, it's time to get back on your post and fulfil your God given purpose!

> *"Cheap people know the price of everything, but the value of nothing." — Oscar Wilde*

CHAPTER 6

Fear Has Lost, Faith Has Won

ON AUGUST 26, 2015, a flawed judicial system caged my youngest son like an animal for a false imprisonment charge. A prejudiced judge saw it fit to not allow him to exercise his first-time offender rights. His case went to a jury trial, and per the jury instructions, "confined and detained" was noted, which made it difficult to reach a verdict. The jury foreman asked the judge for the law definition of "confined and detained." Because a law definition could not be found, the judge modified the jury instructions, changing the "and" to an "or."

The judge declined my son's defense attorney the opportunity to reclose arguments, and forty-five minutes later, the jury rendered a verdict, finding him guilty. I had to watch three officers handcuff my 150-pound son, slowly walking him out of the courtroom. I lost my will to live. Due to a miscarriage of justice, the judge sentenced him to ten years, to serve seven.

During his incarceration, while faced with physical attacks, he made it his goal to publish his first book *Spir'it-ual Ar'chi-tec'ture* in October of 2016. My son reminds me of Apostle Paul, whom God chose for a special mission (2 Tim. 2:9.)

The judicial system saw fit to imprison him on a charge of "False Imprisonment" for a period of 10 years/to serve 7, being in a toxic relationship with his girlfriend (who at the time, he loved very much), but God separated him from his family from August 26, 2015 to February

6, 2018 because He had a purpose for his life, and the enemy knew it. You may be asking the question, "Why was he (my son) persecuted and imprisoned as a first-time offender?"

He, like Apostle Paul, suffered all these things because he had a calling on his life. God loves us, but because of our sinful nature, He allows these things to happen. He knows that by allowing us to experience failure, pain, and struggle, we will grow stronger in our faith, become closer to Him, and move away from sin. Just because we are benevolent followers of Jesus, doesn't mean we are exempt from hardship. The enemy never hits what he doesn't want. For example: he doesn't want your car, he can't drive it!

God allows for struggling and pressure to build our inner strength and faith.

On June 10, 2018, my son accepted his calling into ministry, rendering his first sermon in the church where he grew up attending.

Before & After

God's Transformation

CHAPTER 7

Freedomversary, Forever Thankful

"He calls His own sheep by name and leads them out"
– John 10:3

You see, on my birthday I was born.

God gave me life.

He gave me breath.

He blessed me with two beautiful gifts.

On August 26, 2015 I got the wind knocked out of me.

On February 6, 2018, I was resuscitated back to life.

My youngest son got his life back.

He not only gained wisdom he got his freedom back.

God gave him another chance after we thought his life was over.

Like the prodigal son, he was sent away at the age of twenty-two.

Not knowing what to expect, he tried to mentally prepare himself for what was to come.

He felt his life was over.

And everything he worked for:

Going to school, getting a great job, leaving that six-figure income because he knew his worth was bigger than working eighty hours a week building another person's dream.

He obtained a real estate license.

In the midst of building a fashion brand, everything was snatched.

At first, I didn't understand.

I kept asking God, "Why my son?"

I heard a sweet, soft voice say, "God has to have alone time with him."

So, yes, he was placed in the middle of nowhere doing real-deal time, but it was more like a spiritually intense bootcamp.

He turned a negative into a positive and became an author.

He wrote and published his first book and completed his second book while away.

His mind was set on sitting down for an extensive period of time.

He read over 300 books.

He became a mentor to so many individuals around him because he was looked up to for rising up through adversity.

He had to immediately adapt to an environment that didn't have his back.

Twenty-three hours in a small, boxed-in room.

The food tasted beyond horrible.

Everyone who he thought was in his corner forgot about him on the outside.

His mail was read before it was given to him.

Bend over, squat, and cough cavity checks.

Loss of privacy.

He was now considered "someone else's property," having to watch his back twenty-four-seven.

God was just equipping him because His plans were a lot different than the time he was given.

He ended up doing a little shy of three years.

He was reborn.

So, a lot of people ask him, "How are you so motivated daily?"

His response is: "The individual who opened the final gate for me to my freedom told me that I would be back.

I laughed and told him we'll see."

It's a proven fact that God won't put more on you than you can bear.

He was built for the challenge and test.

God equips His soldiers for battle.

You may be going through something, and you have no idea why.

Realign your posture, pivot, and stay positive.

There's always a positive that lies on the other side of a negative.

My son made a pact with God that he would impact over a million people worldwide.

So, the type of work he does now is impacting God's people globally.

God may not send you away, but He will sit you down and isolate you from everything.

Happy Freedomversary to you, my baby boy.

I know that you'll continue to push the mission.

All he walked out with was an oversized white t-shirt, khaki pants, plain white sneakers, a white fabric net bag with paperwork, letters he received in the mail, and a twenty-five-dollar prepaid card.

Today, God has blessed him with way more than just a net bag.

"Jesus took the blows because we're worth the sacrifice."

CHAPTER 8

The Voice of Faith is Calling You, Answer Him!

HEARING OUR NAME spoken makes an impression on us, one way or another. Whenever my mother asked in an authoritative voice, "Regina Mone'a, do you hear me talking to you?" I knew she wasn't calling my name if she didn't need anything. Hearing "Regina Mone'a" in her thunderous tone as I strode from my bedroom into the kitchen had a very different feel.

Names convey a sense of who we are and how others relate to us.

Now, let's dig a little deeper!

It's like this: knowing what faith is, is one thing. Exercising faith and putting it to work is something else.

You may feel worried. It may seem like it's never going to happen. But don't verbalize it. Stop holding on to your sickness and the naysayers comments to you. Don't get trapped by your words.

In life, there are always two voices fighting for your attention. You'll hear a voice of defeat saying, "It's never going to work out." But, if you listen carefully, you'll hear the voice of faith saying, "God has a way; you got this." You get to choose which voice comes to life by what you speak. When you verbalize that thought, you're giving it life, and the right to come to pass. You have to get in agreement with God. The voice of defeat may seem louder, but you can override it. You can take away all its power by choosing the voice of faith and remembering the points below:

- Be obedient to what He has told you.
- It's God's calling, not yours.
- Use the gifts and talents given to you.
- Your calling is attached to what you enjoy.
- Be excited and tenacious pursuing your God-given purpose.
- Continue studying the Word.
- Keep around only those people who genuinely want to see you win.
- Eliminate distractions.

Let's Pray:

> *"Father, thank you that I do not have to keep being trapped in worry and defeat by the words of my mouth. I choose to not listen to the voice of doubt, but to listen and obey the voice of faith. Help me to keep speaking the words that are in agreement with what You say. It's in Jesus's precious Name I pray, for I am truly grateful and thankful. Amen."*

CHAPTER 9

Speak Power-Punching, Faith-Filled Words

Words are powerful.

WHEN GOD PUTS a promise in your heart, embrace it. When trouble comes knocking at your door, don't go grabbing your phone trying to call everyone in your contacts. Make prayer and praise your weapon of warfare. Do not dare debate God's Word saying, "I still feel symptoms of Covid." "Those migraine headaches will never go away." "The pain in my neck and my back will never go away." Whatever you verbally put out into the atmosphere that does not align up with God's Word will take over your life. Whatever you sow, you will reap. Flip the script in your way of thinking and get into the habit of boldly speaking faith-filled words.

In a praying church, God always confirms His Word. Step out in faith and allow Him to be God. If you want to experience God's power, you have to be in sync and in tune, so that He can do what He was called to do. If you don't know the value of prayer, you will never experience the benefits and power.

"Lord, thank You that I am healed. Be it unto me even as You have said."

God will never twist and turn the truth to fit our circumstances. Let's not be more educated than the level of our obedience.

Let's Pray:

> *"Father, thank you for Your promise to Mary that she had found favor with You, and she would give birth to Your Son. Thank you that no Word from You has ever returned void. I believe that I am highly favored, and Your words to me will be fulfilled. In Jesus's precious Name, I pray, for I am truly grateful and thankful. Amen."*

> *"Shift your thoughts and watch what comes out of your mouth." — Daniel Handler*

CHAPTER 10

I Will Not Stay at Ground Zero Because I'm a Seed Thrower

WHEN WE FACE life's challenges, it's easy to become bitter, negative, or selfish, where all we think about is, "My problems, my illness, my pain, my bills, my loneliness." Here's a fun fact: as long as we're only focused on ourselves, we will stay stuck at ground zero.

In our time of need, we have to learn to sow a seed. In order to get what you want; you have to give away what you need. If you need happiness, don't sit around in self-pity. Do yourself a favor be a good Samaritan and make somebody else happy. God will use that seed to bring you joy. If you need better health, help somebody else get well. If you want God to solve your problems, take your mind off yourself and help solve somebody else's problem. The bottom line is that you have to give away what you need.

Now, this goes against human nature. If I'm discouraged, I want you to cheer me up. If I'm struggling in my finances, I don't want to bless you. I want you to bless me. But it works just the opposite. When God sees you getting outside of yourself, when He sees you being good to somebody in the midst of your own struggles, when He sees you cheering up a friend even though you're in the midst of a catastrophic event, or when He sees you praying for somebody to get well -- even though you don't feel well -- that's the seed that God will use to bring a harvest back into your own life.

It's that simple. You can't solve your own problem, but you can solve somebody else's problem. You can't figure out what you should do, but you can tell a friend exactly what they should do. God will enable you to help others. If you sow a seed and help others, that's what is going to bring your own harvest. When you reach out and give of your own time, your energy, and you pray for people and encourage someone, the seed that holds your problem's answer is being watered. It's taking root.

Let's Pray:

> *Dear Heavenly Father, I will run the course You have set before me. Help me to see where I have gotten off course. Be a lamp unto my feet and a light unto my path. Help me to not miss the mark. Show me how to run my race in ways that bring pleasure to You. In the name of Jesus, I submit this prayer to you. Amen.*

CHAPTER 11

He Just Wants Your Yes!

WHEN YOU PURCHASE property (after the mortgage lender runs and determines your credit is worthy enough to go to closing), you have to make a large down payment. In order to keep the house from going into foreclosure, you must make smaller monthly payments by the due date per your signed contract. You can't change your mind and say, "I don't feel like making payments. I'll pay my mortgage whenever I feel like it" without serious consequences.

The same truth applies to your relationship with God. To make Him your permanent dwelling place, your initial down payment is required in making Him #1 in your life. After that, ongoing payments must be made, which means saying yes whenever God directs you to do something. They are all a part of the purchase; one happens initially, and the other is eternally ongoing (like mortgage payments).

The Lord will only give as much payment to me as I am willing to give to Him. I can possess only as much of what He has for me, and as I am willing to secure with my obedience.

God gives answers in 3 ways:

> He says *yes* and gives you what you want.
> He says *no* and gives you something better.
> He says *wait* and gives you the *best*.

Since I was a child, I always wanted to be a successful pianist. It has always been my desire and drive to demonstrate my work of art in front of my church. Nevermind the fact that I possibly didn't have what it took to accomplish this goal. After I accepted the Lord as my personal Savior, the Holy Spirit impressed upon my heart to develop an intimate relationship with Him, and to accept and walk into my purpose. I accepted my calling and began singing and directing my church choir. One of my favorite songs I used to sing was "In the Midst of It All" by Yolanda Adams. Every time I sang that song, the Holy Spirit would not only take over my vocals, but He also had me on the best spiritual high!

At the conclusion of the song, I ended up laying prostrate on my knees, giving Him reverence for all He has done for me.

The part we don't want to hear is that there will come a time when each of us must place our desires and dreams in the hands of God, so that He will show up and show out in our lives. In other words, get out of your own way and let God have His way in your life. If you've always had a certain picture of what you think you should do, you have to be willing to let that picture be destroyed. If it really is what God wants for you, He will raise you up to do that and more. If it isn't, you will be frustrated as long as you cling to it.

Often times, the desires of your heart are the desires of His heart, but they still must be achieved His way, not yours. Furthermore, you must know that it is He who is accomplishing them in you; you're not achieving them yourself. God wants us to stop holding on to our dreams and start holding on to Him, so that He can enable us to soar above our own limitations. Whenever we let go of what we long for, God will bring it back to us in another dimension.

THE BLESSING IN THE QUICK RESPONSE

Saying yes to God means being willing to obey Him immediately when we hear His voice, and not waiting until all else fails or we feel like we're at the edge of the slope. For God to transform us into being whole, we have to be totally available to Him. If He is telling us "*do this,*" then our reply should be, "*Yes, God.*" This will bring the desired results more quickly.

> *"Your breakthrough will manifest when you get in position and pivot."*

CHAPTER 12

Speak Up Child, Whatever You Need is in the Room!

"STOP GOING INTO the room taking selfies when you should be taking notes. Inherit the experience."

Here's a fun fact: The world around us is in total and complete chaos!

But guess what, are you going to lose yourself in the midst of all the news you hear on television or on the radio?

Are you going to consume yourself with all the negativity around you?

Are you calling someone in your phone contacts to gossip about what someone said on your social media page?

In a twenty-four-hour day, how much time are you spending on social media, on the phone, watching television, and listening to secular music on the radio?

When you wake up in the morning, what is the first thing you do?

During the course of the day, do you go to a quiet space and talk to God?

Do you find yourself entertaining negative people who love to complain?

Have you lied and disrespected someone you said you love (i.e., your spouse, your sibling, your coworker, your neighbor?)

Here's a fact check: we all have to stand before God on Judgement Day and face all the wrong we've done to each other.

Anything that we are holding on to or faced with, we can go to God in prayer. Yes, you can pray anywhere, and you should. But there is something about going to a place where you are alone, just you and God, with no distractions. Find a place that allows you to speak to Him, and be real about everything that's on your heart, where it's quiet enough to hear His voice.

As a mother, wife, career woman and entrepreneur, I never set aside an acceptable amount of time in a day to pray and read the Bible in peace. However, when I saw the movie, *War Room*, my heart was compelled to find a place where I could get real with God!

Before your time expires, go into a quiet place where there's no distractions, and turn off your phone, television, and radio. Go to God in prayer and repent. Have a conversation with Him – simply unload everything before Him. He's waiting and wants to hear from you. Relax, release, and rejoice!

Override the way you feel and do what you were called to do. The art of it is not to kill the voice; the art is to turn down the volume and build an intimate relationship with Him. Find the true power of being you. The Word of God needs no crutches. If you're not sure what your purpose is, go to God in prayer. The greatest sermon lies within you!

> *"Get into position, pivot, and ask God for whatever it*
> *is that you need. Then leave your request at the altar."*

CHAPTER 13

I Need to Talk to You Jesus, So I Know How to Swing My Sword

I HAVE NEVER been a confrontational person. As a child, if someone disrespected or threatened me, I knew who to unload them on *my siblings*. Listen, I wasn't a punk, I just didn't embrace confrontation. It's that simple.

If you're experiencing issues with your neighbor, coworker, manager, church member, or relative, don't go grabbing your phone to call someone for advice; call Jesus! Listen, the government is no longer church friendly. There's going to come a time when the government will try to stop us from prayer, praise, and worship. Make God bigger than your problem. When life hits you, don't keep praying your problems back to God! Once you give Him your problems, leave them there before Him. Now, let's talk about the enemies in your life. There are people who can't stand you; they're praying for your downfall. God will use them to feed you all the blessings you deserve. Your enemies are a part of your destiny. As such, God will use your enemies to get you to your blessing. Where is the raven getting the bread and meat? 1 Kings 17:2-16

From your enemy's palace! So, your enemy might as well get comfortable supplying your meal, because they cannot and will not stop the raven from taking their food to give to you.

In the midst of your mess, God will push you through the finish line; just stay in faith. We've got all this power available to us. So, my question to you is: How much of this power are you using? If it's His will, it's His bill; now, let that marinate. He always reveals Himself through His Word. We've got to learn obedience, in the midst of our suffering, just like Jesus was obedient in the midst of His suffering. Remember, God sees everything, and He knows exactly what we need, when we need it, and He will provide it to us at the right and appointed time!

Sometimes, the will of God will take you places you don't want to be. No matter how intense and unbearable your situation gets, do not conform to this world!

> *"The higher God takes you; the enemy will make it his goal to stay on your toes!"*

CHAPTER 14

I'm Speaking My Breakthrough. Are You?

WHEN MY YOUNGEST son was away from his family for almost three years, I nearly threw in the towel. I felt like I was having an out-of-body experience. I started sinking, and the breath of life was slowly leaving my body. I literally thought I was dying. Then I heard an inner, sweet, soft voice tell me, "*Your baby boy is ok. I am with him, I never left his side, and I never will. Just trust Me and rest my child – victory is yours.*"

Tears flowed down my face like water coming out of a water faucet. It was like God had spiritually resuscitated me back to life!

Listen, a breakthrough requires you to have the courage and strength to stop settling for second best. Everything you need in your life is contingent upon what comes out of your mouth. The problem is that your mind is blocking you from seeing the breakthrough and success tools that you need to navigate your life into the right direction. If you are not going through a low point, then you are not in need of a breakthrough; you just need encouragement.

If God is a difference and a game changer in your life, move forward with your God-given purpose and declare someone else's breakthrough. Do not only pray for yourself, pray for others.

What are you going to do with what God has given you?

Will you be the answer to someone else's prayer?

It's like this: what you did or what you're doing did not stop God's plan and purpose for your life. To get something you've never had, you have to get out of your own way, and open up your mouth, declaring and decreeing that whatever you need "is yours." God gives you enough for only today. Stop worrying about tomorrow; God's got that covered.

> *"Lord, prepare me to be a sanctuary for the lost, the broken, and wayward soul."*

Have you ever asked yourself this question, why am I here? Here is a fun fact, God has given each one of us a purpose. When you find out your WHY and your PURPOSE, you no longer sit in a place of complacency. So, I implore you to run your race, remember to sow, and grab some quotes along the way.

"If you have a need
sow a seed."
— John Barrett

"God is moved by your faith, not your fear; now walk in it."

"You have to:
Initiate the blessing…
Initiate the healing…
Initiate the favor…"

"God doesn't stay
in a state of anger;
He stays in a space
of grace."

"Whatever you tune into, you turn into." – Rico McDaniel

"Stop letting people run all over you. Speak the truth, own the room, and watch your enemies be uncomfortable."

"You are allowed to change the price of what it costs to access you." – Melanie Curtis

"Whatever you've been praying for is in the room."

"Fear is gone.
Victory is won."

"Our heavenly
Father hears;
He's in the room."

"Stay in your lane."

"God did *not* appoint you judge, jury, and prosecutor."

"You have six months to mind your own business, and six months to leave everyone else's business alone."

"God is not a mathematical problem for you to solve. He is a wonderful counselor, mighty God, everlasting Father, Prince of Peace."

"Stop stressing and
start striving."

"Swing your sword,
so that you can put
the enemy to flight."

"Don't be a copy of someone else's original form."

"The Word of God
needs no crutch."

"The farther you push a person to their destiny, the higher you go."

"The wisdom you're looking for is found in the Word of God."

"Every morning that you wake up, be ready to learn."

"Stop going into the room taking selfies, when you should be taking notes."

"All of your ancestors and forefathers are counting on you."

"You can't stop me
from dreaming,
no matter how
hard you try."

"People don't care
how much you know;
they want to know
how much you care."
Theodore Roosevelt

"Whatever entertains you, trains you."
Now, let that marinate!"
Toby Brown

"We can't blame
a person for not
knowing what they
don't know."

"When you know more prayer, you inherit more power."

"God = Strength
Your
Problem = Weak."

"The same God that gave you the vision for your business, will give you the clients."

"We've got to learn Faith and obedience, in the midst of our suffering, just like Jesus was Faithful and obedient in the midst of His suffering."
"Stop fooling yourself; God sees everything."

"Sometimes, the Will of God will take you places you don't want to be."

"Wait...
are you in position?
If not, stop wasting
God's time, and get
in position, before
it's too late."

"Godly counsel
and wisdom are
paramount."

"Sickness and disease cannot dwell in the same place God dwells."

"God fills us to use us."

"You can't feel God's presence without a foundation of prayer."

"If you want to experience God's power, you have to be in sync and in tune, so that He can do what He was called to do."

"If you don't know the value of prayer, you will never experience the benefits and power."

"God never intended
His children to
live paycheck to
paycheck."

"If you want to be in the over-flow, you have to be intentional with your sowing."

"If you don't stop holding on to your past, you're going to wreck!"

"It's ok to copycat, just copy the right cat."

"Warning comes before destruction, and there's no compromising in that."

"Pay off your debt before it buries you alive."

"You'll never become wealthy chasing money; let the money chase you."

"Get your credit and finances in order, so that you can be a lender, and not a borrower."

"You can't lead if
you're not willing
to follow."

"Those who neg-
atively talk about
you for no reason
want to occupy
space in your world
and success."

"Self-centered
=
Self-destruction."

"You are to be a con-
duit of kindness
to others."

"You cannot have access to the harvest, if you are not willing to sow."

"Success minus speed

=

deficit."

"Your comfort zone
is a trap owned by
the enemy."

"If you are walking through a season and don't know how to navigate, stop and pivot."

"If you want to be a recipient of positive change, replace your friends with account-ability partners."

"Negative energy
will keep you at
ground zero...
wait for it, wait for it!"

"Success is not for the lazy and complacent; it's for those that are willing to pay the price to obtain it."

"Stop wasting your time on people who continues to give life to their sickness, not realizing they will never get healed."

"Duplication is the fertilizer to success."

"Jesus said, 'The things you see Me do, I want you to do the same."
Luke 5:5

"People will buy you when you're high and sell you when you're low."

"Wealth is obtained not by how much money you make; it's by how much money you keep."
- Denzel Washington

"If you want to grow people, you've got to put them in the environment from where you grew."

"Do you have LOL –
Layers
of
Leadership
— in your arsenal?"

"When the mentor shows up in your life, don't blow it!"

"Unmerited Favor that you don't deserve is coming into your life."

"What's snagging your clothes? What are some of the negative things you're holding on to?"

"Get your heart right,
and
God will change your
situation."

"Are you alone walking through a season of financial lack, and don't know how to navigate?"

"You can't tell me anything, unless you've walked in it."

"Stop hanging with negativity and worry and get with grace and mercy!"

"When you walk into the room, you shift it."

"You are a genera-
tional curse breaker!"

"You attract what you are, instead of what you want."

"Let's push each other into the break-through, instead of a breakdown."

"Going from ratchet to righteous."

"Women, you want to know why God hasn't given you your Boaz? – Ruth 1:16 Because you keep messing with those Bozos!"

"Man's rejection was God's protection."

"As long as you're holding onto the doorknob, God can't move you through a bigger door."

"Stop giving CPR to dead situations!"

"God is waiting on
you to pivot."

"God is my only acceptable compromise."

"Being broke is all
a part of this game
called life.
Staying broke is
some personal stuff."

"Stay in position, so you don't have to worry about getting into position."

"God gives us free
will to create and
execute our plans."

"Your godly presence makes temptation lose its power."

"You're about to win big right in front of the people who counted you out!"

"Ya'll better stop treating God like He's an option... we need Him in everything we do!"

"I'm not looking for friends; I'm looking for accountability partners."

"I lead by example,
not by advice!"

"Focus on the process, and not the outcome."

"God not only cares about your relation-ship with Him, but He also cares about your relationship with others."

"Trouble is inevitable, but misery is optional."

"God can do what medical science can't do!"

"God is going to use your few minutes of turbulence to your advantage."

"Relax, be patient and wait for God to give you the desires of your heart."

"Give your dreams
and desires
over to God."

"In every battle you face, stop trying to be right! Exercise your peace instead."

"Your imagination of me in your mind is your responsibility, not mine."

"Learn to throw your problems in the trash."

"You'll never win being deceitful."

"If you replace your friends with account-ability partners, you'll grow."

CPSIA information can be obtained
at www.ICGtesting.com
Printed in the USA
BVHW020123150522
637041BV00027B/302